INSIDE BATTLE MACHINES
SUBMARINES

American submarine pioneer John Holland in one
of his submarines in 1899 (see pp.10–11)

by Chris Oxlade

HUNGRY
TOMATO.

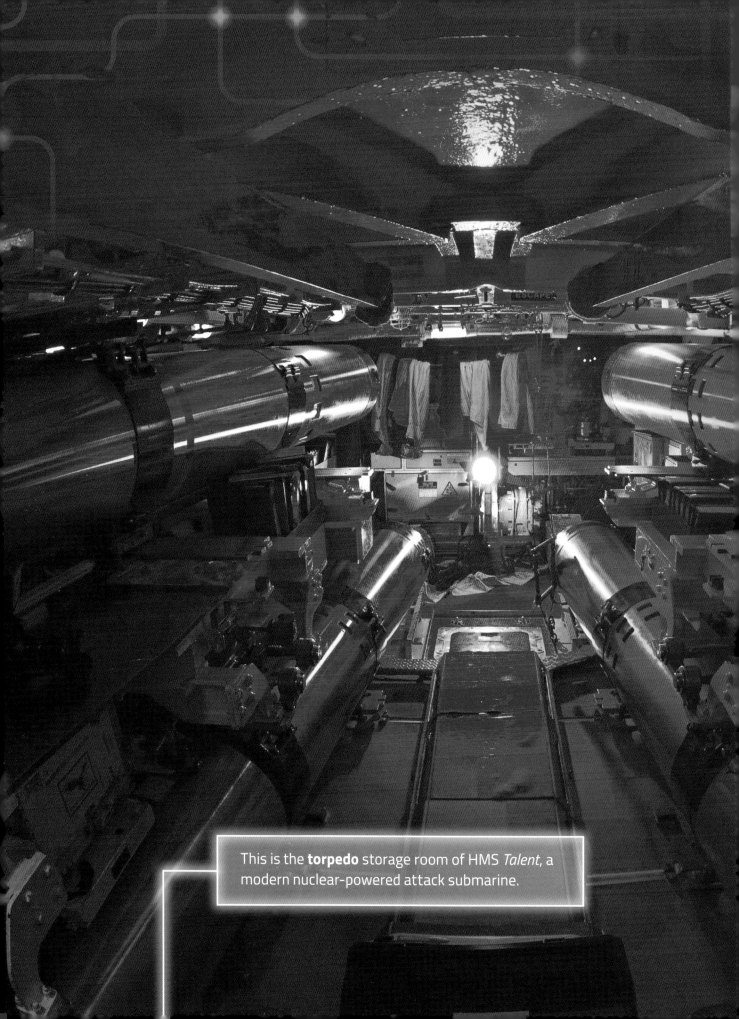

This is the **torpedo** storage room of HMS *Talent*, a modern nuclear-powered attack submarine.

Contents

[Highlighted words appear in the glossary]

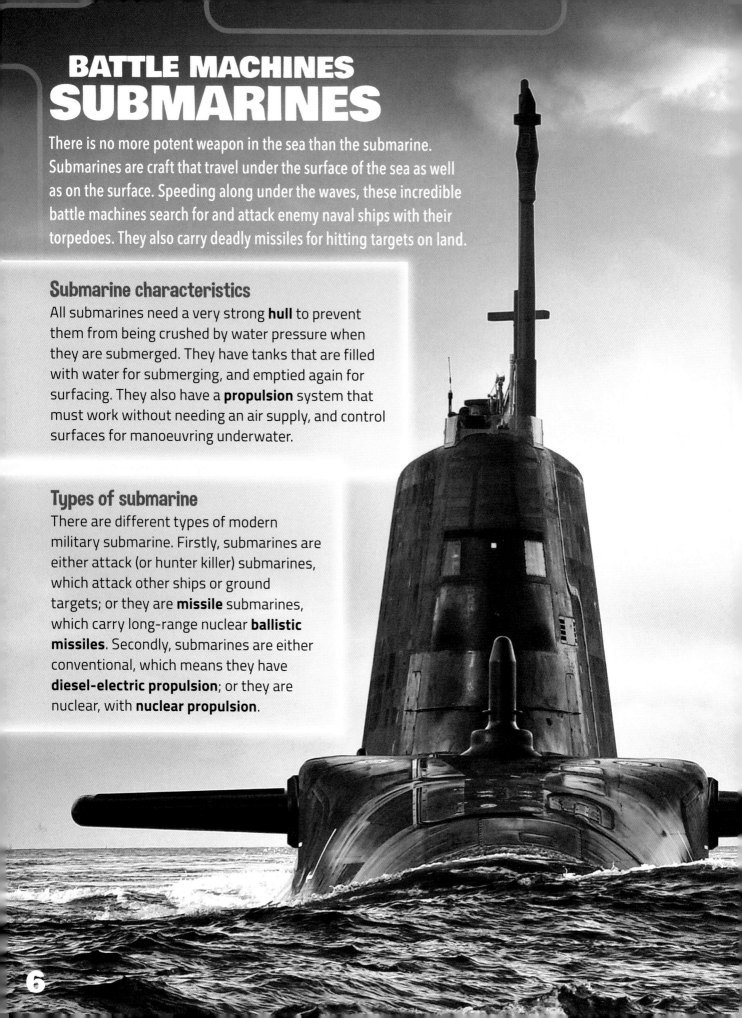

BATTLE MACHINES
SUBMARINES

There is no more potent weapon in the sea than the submarine. Submarines are craft that travel under the surface of the sea as well as on the surface. Speeding along under the waves, these incredible battle machines search for and attack enemy naval ships with their torpedoes. They also carry deadly missiles for hitting targets on land.

Submarine characteristics

All submarines need a very strong **hull** to prevent them from being crushed by water pressure when they are submerged. They have tanks that are filled with water for submerging, and emptied again for surfacing. They also have a **propulsion** system that must work without needing an air supply, and control surfaces for manoeuvring underwater.

Types of submarine

There are different types of modern military submarine. Firstly, submarines are either attack (or hunter killer) submarines, which attack other ships or ground targets; or they are **missile** submarines, which carry long-range nuclear **ballistic missiles**. Secondly, submarines are either conventional, which means they have **diesel-electric propulsion**; or they are nuclear, with **nuclear propulsion**.

First nuclear submarine

This is the crew of the world's first nuclear submarine, the **USS** *Nautilus*, which was launched in 1958. The crew are in the control room, concentrating hard as *Nautilus* travels under the polar ice pack.

Astute-class submarine

Length: 97 metres

Beam: 11 metres

Displacement: 7,000 tonnes

Propulsion: nuclear reactor

Top speed: 56 kilometres per hour

Crew: 98

Dive depth: 300 metres

Weapons: Spearfish torpedoes / Tomahawk cruise missiles

Modern nuclear attack submarine

This is **HMS** *Ambush*, an **Astute-class** submarine of the British Royal Navy, travelling on the surface. HMS *Ambush* is a state-of-the-art nuclear-powered attack submarine, armed with torpedoes and **cruise missiles**.

The first submarine that we know actually existed was built around 1620, but it's likely that shipbuilders had talked about the idea of underwater boats before then. There is a written record of a submarine in 1578. Early submarines used materials and marine technology of the time, such as wood, leather and oars.

Drebbel's submarine

Naval historians think that the first submarine was built by a Dutch inventor called Cornelis Drebbel in about 1620. Drebbel's craft was like a rowing boat with a lid on top, made of wood and covered with leather to make it waterproof. Oars that stuck out through leather flaps propelled it. This submarine made many trips up and down the River Thames in London, diving four or five metres under the surface.

Bushnell's *Turtle*

This peculiar egg-shaped craft was the first submarine to go into battle. It was built by American inventor David Bushnell. There was just enough space for the operator to sit inside. Around him were controls for diving, surfacing and steering, and a hand crank to turn the propeller

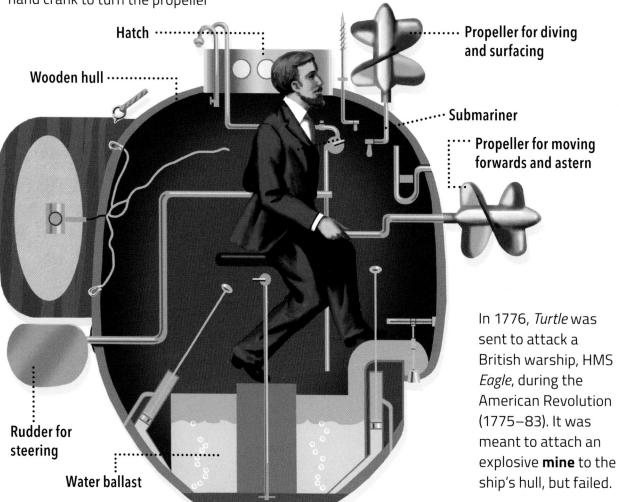

Hatch

Wooden hull

Propeller for diving and surfacing

Submariner

Propeller for moving forwards and astern

Rudder for steering

Water ballast

In 1776, *Turtle* was sent to attack a British warship, HMS *Eagle*, during the American Revolution (1775–83). It was meant to attach an explosive **mine** to the ship's hull, but failed.

Modern reproduction of
Drebbel's submarine

Nautilus

Robert Fulton was a famous American inventor. He designed a submarine that he built
in France in 1801, called *Nautilus*. It had an iron frame covered with copper sheets,
and a collapsing mast and sail to take advantage of any wind. Four crew members
operated the machine, turning the propeller by hand. Like the earlier *Turtle*, *Nautilus*
was supposed to attack ships by creeping up to them and attaching an explosive mine.
However, when it tried to sink some
British battleships, it couldn't muster
the speed to catch up with them.

Turtle

Length: 3 metres

Beam: 90 centimentres

Height: 1.8 metres

Crew: 1

Weapons: explosive charge

Top speed: 5 kilometres per hour

HUNLEY AND HOLLAND

Despite the attacks on ships by submarines in the late 18th century, it wasn't until the 1860s that a submarine actually sank a ship for the first time. The submarine was the *H. L. Hunley*, which fought for the Confederate side in the American Civil War. It was one of several experimental submarines tried out in the war.

H. L. Hunley

This submarine was named after Horace Hunley, who paid for it to be built. *H. L. Hunley* was just 12 metres long – a metal tube with flattened ends. The crew propelled the submarine with a crank that turned the propeller. The dangerous nature of early submarines was demonstrated when *H. L. Hunley* sank three times, killing its crew, including Hunley. It was recovered each time and in 1864 sank a Union ship, using an explosive charge on the end of a long pole. But the explosion also damaged the submarine, and it sank for a final time.

Holland's submarine

Submarine designers tried out different forms of power. They found that steam engines could not be used while submerged, and that the batteries on electric motors ran out quickly. The invention of the internal-combustion (IC) engine solved these problems. In 1897 in the United States, John Holland completed a design of his own. *Holland* had electric motors powered by batteries for use submerged, and a gasoline IC engine for use on the surface. The engine also recharged the batteries. The US Navy bought the submarine, and the British Royal Navy ordered five more. *Holland* is thought of as the first modern-style submarine.

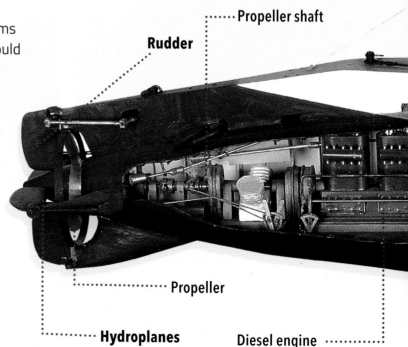

Propeller shaft

Rudder

Propeller

Hydroplanes

Diesel engine

Torpedoes

The torpedo is the submarine's main weapon for attacking ships. A torpedo is like a missile that travels through water. It has a motor to drive it along and an explosive warhead that blows up on contact with a ship. The torpedo was invented by British engineer Robert Whitehead. His first successful torpedo, built in 1866, was about 4 metres long and travelled at about 12 kilometres per hour. It was originally designed to be fired from surface ships.

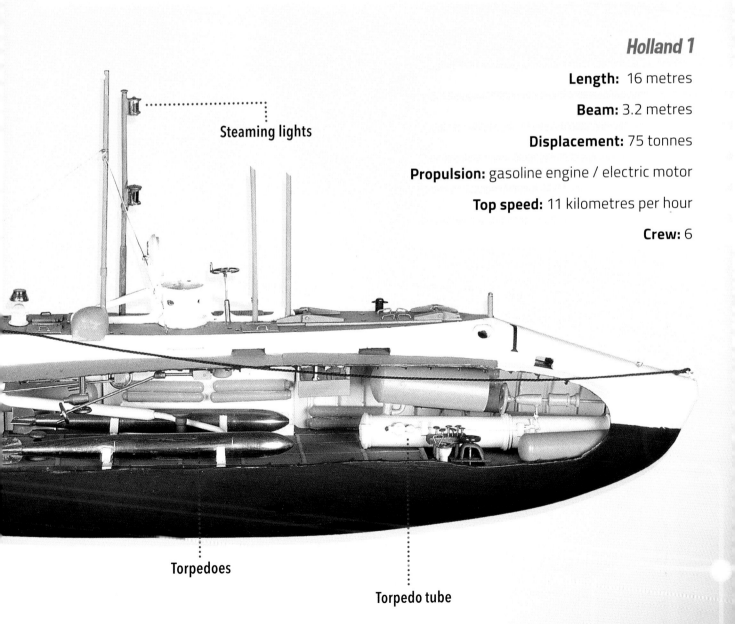

Holland 1

Length: 16 metres

Beam: 3.2 metres

Displacement: 75 tonnes

Propulsion: gasoline engine / electric motor

Top speed: 11 kilometres per hour

Crew: 6

Steaming lights

Torpedoes

Torpedo tube

WORLD WAR I SUBMARINES

Most navies had some small submarines when World War I broke out in 1914. At first nobody really knew how to use submarines in battle, but by the end of the war submarines had had a major impact, sinking thousands of ships. They were used mostly for attacking enemy cargo ships, but they were also used to lay mines, and attack enemy submarines.

Submarine forces

Germany and Britain built up large submarine fleets during World War I. At the start of the war, Germany had 29 submarines, or U-boats (U-boat is from 'undersea boat' – *Unterseeboot* in German). Some are seen here in 1914 in Kiel harbour. The British warship HMS *Pathfinder* was the first ship to be sunk by a torpedo fired from a submarine: the German *U-21*. Of the 351 U-boats built, 178 were sunk, but U-boats sank more than 5,000 Allied ships.

Torpedo room

This is the torpedo room of an American submarine, showing torpedoes ready to fire. This sort of torpedo was powered by compressed air, which made the propeller spin. At the far end of the room is the inner door of the torpedo tube. This door was opened to load a torpedo, then closed again. The outer tube door was opened, letting in water, and the torpedo was fired. In World War I, torpedo tubes were also used secretly to lay mines in shipping lanes and ports.

Engine room

This picture shows German sailors inside a U-boat's engine room – which was not a great place to be! It was hot, cramped and stank of oil. Nearly all World War I submarines continued to use a combination of **diesel engines** and electric motors. The engines recharged the batteries while the submarine was on the surface. A few submarines were fitted with **steam turbines** for high speeds on the surface.

Planes from submarines

Just after World War I, the British Navy launched reconnaissance seaplanes from submarines. The submarine HMS *M2* was fitted with a watertight hangar, a catapult-powered launching rail and a crane for aircraft recovery.

SUBMARINES IN
WORLD WAR II

After the success of submarine warfare in World War I, navies, including those of Britain and the United States, continued to improve their submarines. The machines got larger and faster, and they could travel further without needing to refuel. Weapons also improved, so torpedoes became faster and more accurate. During World War II, submarines played a major part in battles in all the world's oceans.

U-boat builders

Germany already had 57 U-boats when it declared war in 1939. Soon Germany had more submarines than any other country. Its main U-boat was the Type VII (see p.16), which was very effective for its small size. The ultimate German U-boat was the Type XXI, which was twice as fast underwater as the Type VII. German U-boats sank more than 2,500 ships during the war.

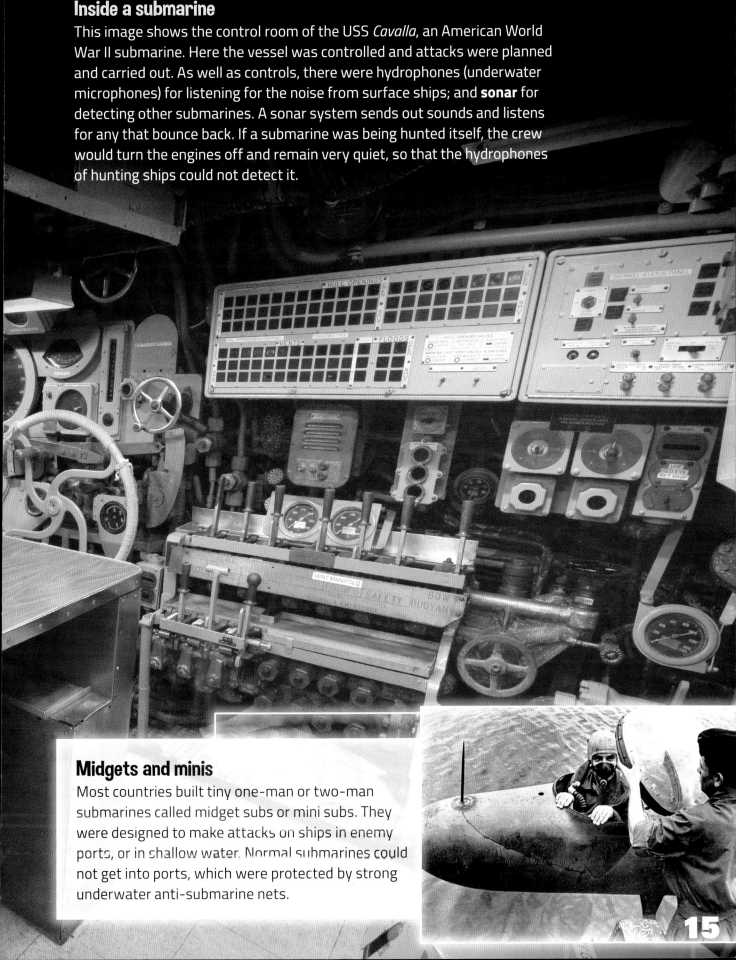

Inside a submarine

This image shows the control room of the USS *Cavalla*, an American World War II submarine. Here the vessel was controlled and attacks were planned and carried out. As well as controls, there were hydrophones (underwater microphones) for listening for the noise from surface ships; and **sonar** for detecting other submarines. A sonar system sends out sounds and listens for any that bounce back. If a submarine was being hunted itself, the crew would turn the engines off and remain very quiet, so that the hydrophones of hunting ships could not detect it.

Midgets and minis

Most countries built tiny one-man or two-man submarines called midget subs or mini subs. They were designed to make attacks on ships in enemy ports, or in shallow water. Normal submarines could not get into ports, which were protected by strong underwater anti-submarine nets.

THE GERMAN U-BOAT

The German navy operated hundreds of U-boats during World War II. Most of these patrolled the North Atlantic, attacking convoys of ships carrying vital supplies between North America and Britain and the Soviet Union.

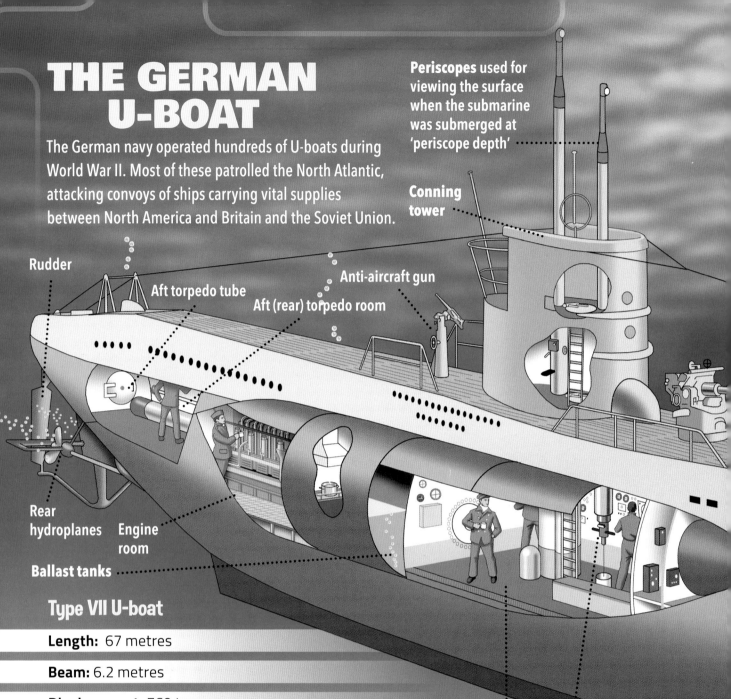

Periscopes used for viewing the surface when the submarine was submerged at 'periscope depth'

Conning tower

Rudder

Aft torpedo tube

Anti-aircraft gun

Aft (rear) torpedo room

Rear hydroplanes

Engine room

Ballast tanks

Control room

Periscopes

Type VII U-boat

Length: 67 metres

Beam: 6.2 metres

Displacement: 769 tonnes

Propulsion: 2 x diesel engines, electric motors

Top speed on surface: 33 kilometres per hour

Top speed submerged: 14 kilometres per hour

Range: 15,700 kilometres

Dive depth: 230 metres

Weapons: torpedoes, mines, main gun, anti-aircraft guns

Crew: 44

Number built: 703

Type VII U-boat

The Type VII U-boat was the most common German U-boat of World War II, and the most common submarine of the war. More than 700 were built. Its weapons were torpedoes, an 88-millimetre deck gun and anti-aircraft guns.

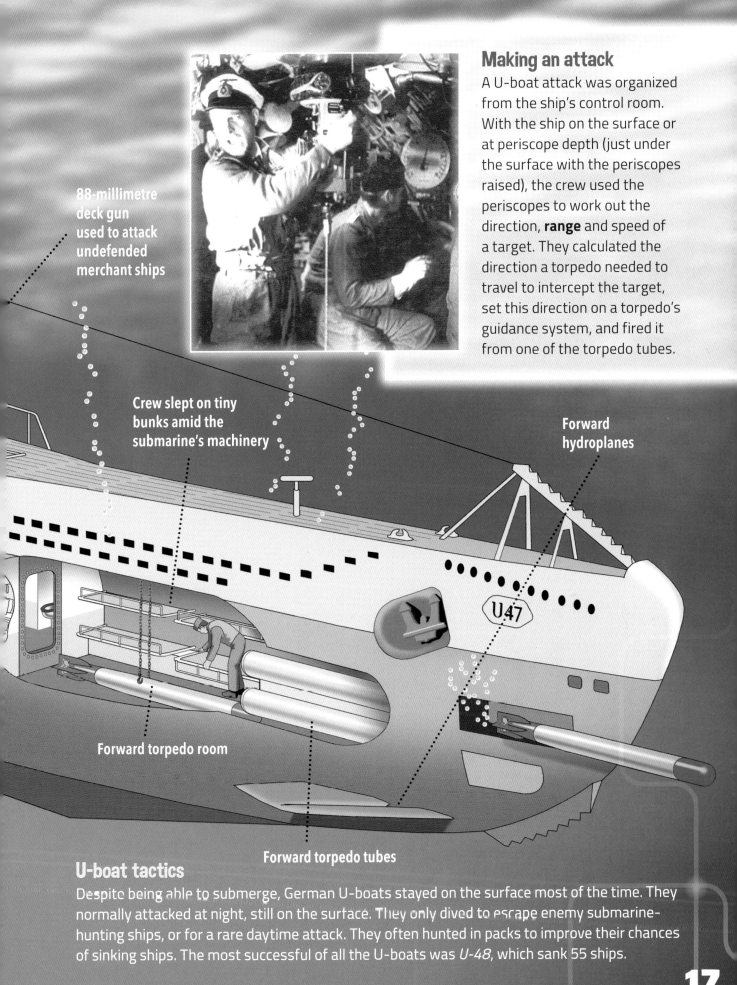

Making an attack

A U-boat attack was organized from the ship's control room. With the ship on the surface or at periscope depth (just under the surface with the periscopes raised), the crew used the periscopes to work out the direction, **range** and speed of a target. They calculated the direction a torpedo needed to travel to intercept the target, set this direction on a torpedo's guidance system, and fired it from one of the torpedo tubes.

88-millimetre deck gun used to attack undefended merchant ships

Crew slept on tiny bunks amid the submarine's machinery

Forward hydroplanes

U 47

Forward torpedo room

Forward torpedo tubes

U-boat tactics

Despite being able to submerge, German U-boats stayed on the surface most of the time. They normally attacked at night, still on the surface. They only dived to escape enemy submarine-hunting ships, or for a rare daytime attack. They often hunted in packs to improve their chances of sinking ships. The most successful of all the U-boats was *U-48*, which sank 55 ships.

NUCLEAR
SUBMARINES

The world of submarines was transformed in the 1950s with the development of the nuclear submarine. In these submarines, a nuclear power plant replaced the diesel-electric system of World War II submarines. This had the massive advantage that the submarines did not have to surface to run their engines, and so could stay submerged almost indefinitely.

First nuclear submarine

USS *Nautilus* of the US Navy was the world's first nuclear-powered submarine. It was an attack submarine launched in 1955. This photograph shows the control room of the second nuclear submarine, USS *Seawolf*, with the US President of the time, Dwight D. Eisenhower, trying out the submarine's periscope.

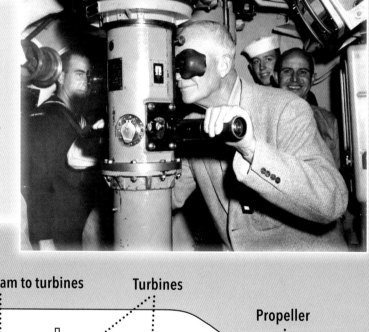

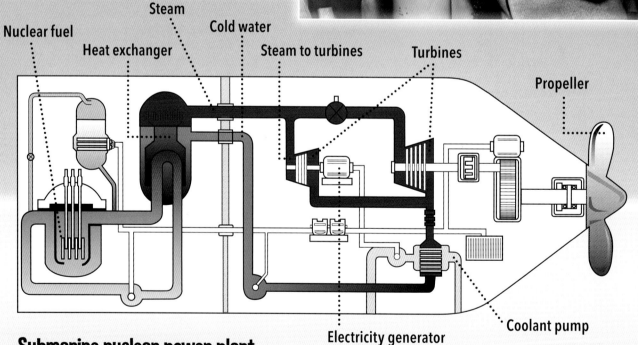

Nuclear fuel • Heat exchanger • Steam • Cold water • Steam to turbines • Turbines • Propeller • Electricity generator • Coolant pump

Submarine nuclear power plant

Most nuclear submarines are powered by a **nuclear reactor** called a pressurized water reactor (PWR). Nuclear reactions in the nuclear fuel give out heat. This heats water around the fuel, which is pumped to a heat exchanger, where it boils water in separate pipes to make steam. The steam is fed to one turbine that turns the propeller, and another turbine that drives a generator to make electricity for the systems and lighting.

Typhoon-class submarine

This huge machine is the biggest submarine ever built, with a displacement of 48,000 tonnes. It's a Russian Akula submarine, called a Typhoon-class by navies in Europe and America. The first was completed in 1981, and only six were built. It carries ballistic missiles.

Typhoon-class submarine

Length: 175 metres

Beam: 23 metres

Displacement: 48,000 tonnes

Power: 2 x nuclear reactors

Top speed surfaced: 41 kilometres per hour

Top speed submerged: 50 kilometres per hour

Dive depth: 400 metres

Crew: 160

Submarines at the North Pole

Because nuclear submarines can stay submerged for long periods of time, they can travel under sea ice. In 1996, USS *Pogy*, a *Sturgeon*-class nuclear submarine, visited the Arctic on a scientific mission to collect samples of water from the Arctic Ocean. It punched its way up through the ice many times during the mission.

MODERN SUBMARINES

Modern submarines are extremely high-tech battle machines. They travel secretly through the oceans, hidden under the surface, always on standby to carry out missions whenever they are needed. Modern submarines have many advanced systems on board, for: navigating; communications (with other ships and its home base); tracking ships, submarines and aircraft; launching and controlling weapons; and defending themselves against attack.

Attack submarine

The smooth, rounded hull of a modern submarine is designed for the submarine to move smoothly while submerged, with minimum water resistance. The hull has a super-strong skin called a pressure hull, which resists water pressure when the submarine dives. The fin, or sail, sticks up from the hull. It houses periscopes, communications aerials and a lookout post. There are torpedo tubes at the bow (front) and stern (rear), and cruise missiles inside the hull.

Submerging and surfacing

The submarine has ballast tanks on each side of the hull. When it's on the surface, the tanks are empty. To dive, the ballast tanks are flooded, making the submarine heavier. Once underwater, hydroplanes are used to steer the submarine up and down through the water. To surface, the ballast tanks are 'blown' by pumping air into them, which pushes the water out.

Crew jobs

The crew of a submarine (known as submariners) are highly trained and work as a tightly knit team. Each crew member has a specific job to do. There are crew who navigate the submarine, weapons experts, communication experts, engineers who operate the nuclear reactors, and crew who look after the other crew, such as cooks.

Repairs and maintenance

Modern submarines are hugely complex machines, crammed with electrical, electronic and mechanical systems. These systems sometimes go wrong, and are fixed by on-board engineers and electricians. The systems also require regular maintenance to keep them working smoothly. Every few years, a submarine returns to base for major maintenance jobs, such as refuelling its nuclear reactor.

Life as a submariner is very different from life as a sailor on a surface ship. For most of their time at sea, modern submarines stay submerged. They can be submerged for months on end, and only surface to re-supply. Conditions on board are cramped, and there is very little contact with the outside world, friends and family.

Working in watches

Inside a submarine deep under the ocean, there's no day or night. A submarine keeps working 24 hours a day, and there are no weekends. The crew of a submarine is divided into teams called watches. Each watch works for a certain number of hours before handing over to the next watch. For example, a watch might work six hours on, then six hours off. Crews regularly practise the drills for making an attack, and for action needed if their submarine is attacked.

Crew space

Submariners have only a small bunk space to call their own, and a small locker in which to store their **kit**. They eat and rest in a small canteen area. Officers have a bit more space, but normally only the captain has an individual cabin.

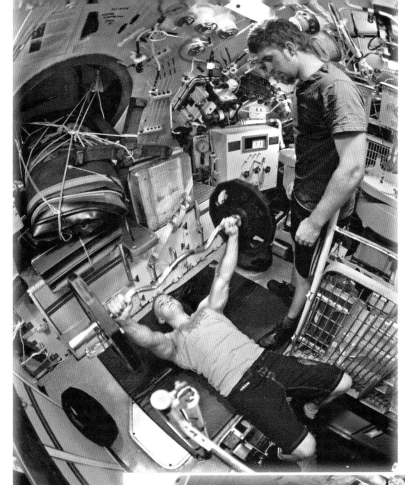

Keeping fit

There's no space to run about and keep fit on a submarine. Submariners keep fit by lifting weights and cycling on exercise bikes. They often have to find any space they can to do their exercise.

Ready for emergencies

There's always a chance that a submarine could be damaged in action, or suffer a mechanical failure, leaving it unable to return to the surface. If the submarine is less than about 200 metres down, the crew can escape using submarine escape immersion equipment (SEIE). They put on a special immersion suit, leave the submarine through a hatch, and float quickly up to the surface. Crews regularly practise for this scenario.

WEAPONS AND DEFENCE

The job of a modern submarine is to attack targets at sea and on land, so a submarine has a range of weapons, including homing torpedoes and missiles. Enemy ships, submarines and aircraft are always searching for submarines. A submarine's main form of defence is to stay deep underwater, but it also has sensing equipment to detect other craft so that it can avoid them.

Ballistic missile launch

Some of the world's countries operate submarines that carry long-range missiles with nuclear **warheads**, known as intercontinental ballistic missiles (ICBMs). The submarines are part of a country's nuclear deterrent: they stay submerged in secret locations, and can launch missiles in case of a nuclear attack, so their presence 'deters' or prevents such an attack.

Rescue submersible

If a submarine is damaged in an enemy attack or accident and sinks in very deep water, a deep submergence rescue vehicle may come to the rescue. The vehicle is a mini submarine. It dives down to the crippled submarine and attempts to dock with it, so that the crew can clamber into it and be carried to the surface.

Tomahawk cruise missile

Warhead of explosives

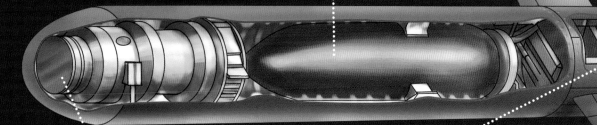

Infra-red guidance system   Fuel cell for electricity supply   Small wings

Submarine sensors

A submarine's main sensors are sonars, which work out the positions of objects in the water. Sonar stands for **so**und **n**avigation **a**nd **r**anging. A sonar system uses sound to detect objects. A passive sonar system detects sounds coming from other ships and submarines. An active sonar system sends out sounds and listens for echoes. The latest submarines have high-resolution cameras and monitors instead of traditional periscopes to view ships on the surface.

Avionics control the missile

Rudders and elevators to change direction, climb and descend

Cruise missiles

A cruise missile is a cross between a missile and an aircraft. After being fired from a submarine using rocket motors, it flies along, powered by a small jet engine, finding its own way to its target, avoiding hills and buildings. A typical cruise missile, such as this Tomahawk, can hit a target a few metres wide after flying more than 1,500 kilometres. Attack submarines can launch cruise missiles from their torpedo tubes while submerged.

Turbojet engine

INSIDE A
SUBMARINE

This is a modern *Virginia*-class submarine of the US Navy. It's a nuclear-powered attack submarine that has been in service since 2004. It carries cruise missiles for hitting land targets, and torpedoes for attacking ships and other submarines. It can also carry a SEAL mini submarine for special-forces operatives. It has a complex array of sonars at the bow, stern and underneath, and a high-resolution light and infra-red sensors.

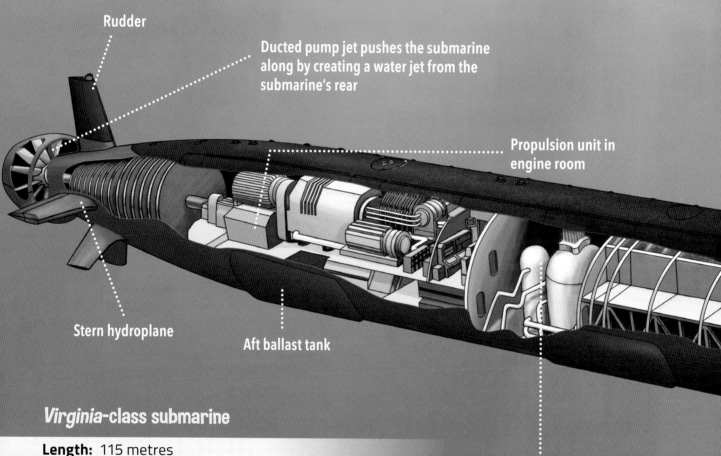

Rudder

Ducted pump jet pushes the submarine along by creating a water jet from the submarine's rear

Propulsion unit in engine room

Stern hydroplane

Aft ballast tank

Nuclear reactor in the reactor compartment

Virginia-class submarine

Length: 115 metres

Beam: 10 metres

Displacement: 7,900 tonnes

Propulsion: nuclear reactor

Top speed: 46 kilometres per hour

Range: unlimited

Dive depth: 240 metres

Crew: 134

Weapons: torpedoes, cruise missiles

In command

This is the commander of the USS *Hawaii*, a *Virginia*-class submarine in service since 2004. It's a nuclear-powered attack submarine. A submarine's commander makes the final decisions about its movements, and when to deploy its weapons. All the submarine's systems are computerized, and information about them is displayed on screens in the control room.

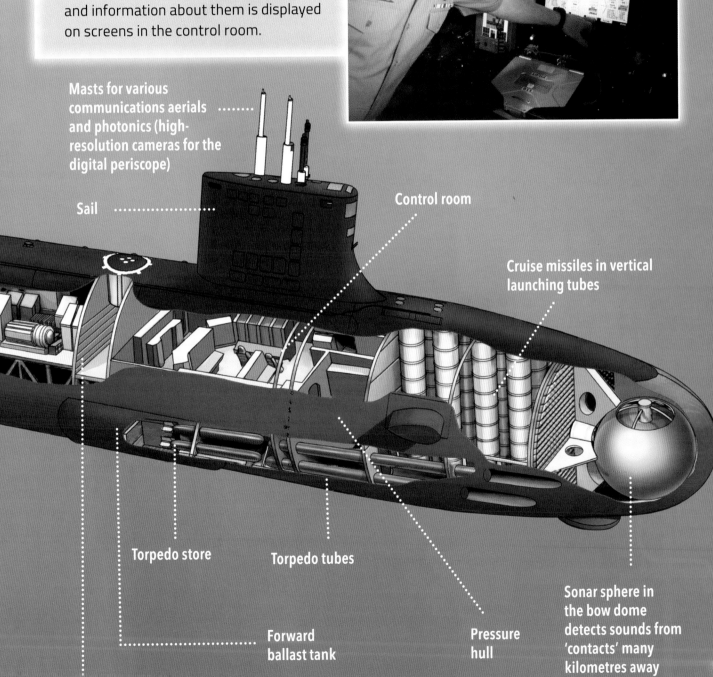

Masts for various communications aerials and photonics (high-resolution cameras for the digital periscope)

Sail

Control room

Cruise missiles in vertical launching tubes

Torpedo store

Torpedo tubes

Forward ballast tank

Pressure hull

Sonar sphere in the bow dome detects sounds from 'contacts' many kilometres away

SEAL lockout trunk, an airlock through which divers can enter and exit the submarine

TIMELINE

4th century BCE
Alexander the Great studies the undersea world from a simple diving bell

1620
Cornelis Drebbel builds the first submarine that we have evidence for, and sailed it along the River Thames in London

1863
The submarine *H. L. Hunley* is launched. It was part of the Confederate naval forces during the American Civil War

1864
H. L. Hunley sinks after attacking and sinking a Union ship. This was the first successful attack by a submarine

1897
American engineer John Holland launches the first submarine to have battery-powered electric motors for travelling submerged, and an internal-combustion engine for use on the surface

1935
The first German Type VII U-boat is launched

1801
Robert Fulton's *Nautilus* is launched. It has a sail for surface travel and a hand crank for submerged travel.

1776
David Bushnell builds *Turtle*, a one-man wooden submarine that makes the first attack of a submarine on another ship

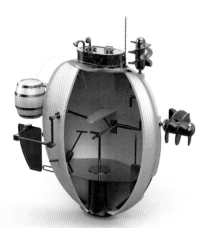

1914-18
Hundreds of submarines take part in World War I

1915
A German submarine sinks the British ocean liner RMS *Lusitania*, on route from New York City to England

1866
British engineer Robert Whitehead invents the torpedo, which goes on to become the main weapon carried by submarines

1939-45
Submarines play a major role in World War II, sinking thousands of naval and civilian ships on both sides

1954
USS *Nautilus*, the world's first nuclear-powered submarine, is launched

(Below) US submariners hoist a torpedo during World War I.

1996
USS *Pogy* goes on a scientific mission under the Arctic sea ice

2004
First American *Virginia*-class submarine enters service

1958
USS *Nautilus* becomes the first submarine to reach the North Pole

FACT FILE

- The most successful of all the German U-boats that operated during World War II was *U-48*. It sank 55 ships. *U-48* survived the war, but was deliberately sunk by its crew to prevent its capture.

- The success of the torpedo that Robert Whitehead designed in the 1860s relied on a clever mechanism that kept it automatically just under the water surface. The mechanism used water pressure to control the torpedo's hydroplane.

- In 1943, two British mini submarines, called X-submarines, attacked Germany's prized battleship *Turpitz* while it was in harbour. One of the submarines placed explosives on *Turpitz*'s hull, which badly damaged the ship.

- In 1958, USS *Nautilus*, the first nuclear-powered submarine, travelled 2,940 kilometres under the Arctic sea ice, visiting the North Pole on the way.

- A modern nuclear sub, such as the British Royal Navy's HMS *Astute*, could stay submerged for 25 years, if needed. Its nuclear fuel lasts that long, and it can produce oxygen for the crew from the seawater.

- Soviet Typhoon-class submarines were the largest submarines ever built. They were named Typhoon by the North Atlantic Treaty Organisation (NATO), during the Cold War in the 1980s. They were actually called Akula-class submarines by the Russians, which means Shark-class.

29

GLOSSARY

Ballistic missile

Astute-class submarine
A type of British submarine using the latest design and technology. In all navies, each design advance brings in a new 'class' of submarine

Ballast tanks
Hollow tanks in the hull of a submarine that are filled with water to make the submarine dive

Ballistic missile
A missile that is launched by a rocket, then falls to its target by gravity

Beam
The width of a ship at its widest point

Conning tower
The tower from where the captain gives orders when the submarine is at the surface

Control surface
A hinged section on the rear edge of a rudder or hydroplane that is moved to control the movement of a submarine

Cruise missile
A missile that flies to its target like a plane, using wings

Diesel engine
A type of internal combustion engine that uses diesel oil as its fuel

Diesel-electric propulsion
A propulsion system where battery powered electric motors are used underwater, and diesel engines are used on the surface. The diesel engines also recharge the batteries

Displacement
A measure of how much a ship weighs

Guided missile
A missile that is guided to its target by a laser or by detecting heat coming from a target

HMS
Short for Her Majesty's Ship, a ship of the British Royal Navy

Hull
The main body of a ship

Hydroplane
A wing-like surface on a submarine that swivels to make the submarine move up or down in the water

Kit
A submariner's clothes and personal belongings

Mine
An explosive device placed underwater that explodes when a ship hits it

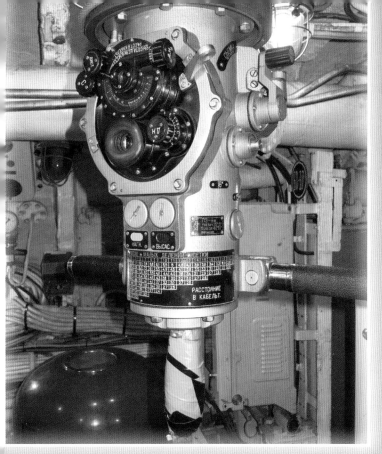
Periscope of a Russian submarine

Missile
A self-propelled weapon that travels through the air to its target

Nuclear propulsion
A propulsion system in which a nuclear reactor creates heat that is used to drive steam turbines that drive propellers

Nuclear reactor
A device that produces heat from nuclear reactions in nuclear fuel

Periscope
An optical device that allows a submarine's crew to see above the surface of the water when the submarine is submerged

Propulsion
The type of engine that makes a ship move, such as a steam turbine, a diesel engine or a nuclear reactor

Range
The distance that a vessel can travel without refuelling; or the distance to a target

Rudder
A flap at the rear for making a ship turn

Sonar
A device that locates objects underwater by sending out sound waves and listening for echoes

Steam turbine
A fan-like rotor that spins when steam flows through it

Submersible
A small, often remote-controlled vessel, that moves under the water

Torpedo
A weapon fired from a ship or submarine that travels through the water to its target

USS
Short for United States Ship, a ship of the US Navy

Warhead
Part of a torpedo or missile that explodes when the missile hits its target

Torpedo room

INDEX

The Author

Chris Oxlade is an experienced author of educational books for children, with more than 200 titles to his name, including many on science and technology. He enjoys camping and adventurous outdoor sports, including rock climbing, hill running, kayaking and sailing. He lives in England with his wife, children and dogs.